For Emily,

M A Stunley

this!

WRITE ME A POEM!

WRITE ME A POEM!

MELODY STARKEY

Matador
Unit E2 Airfield Business Park
Harrison Road, Market Harborough
Leicestershire LE16 7UL
Tel: 0116 279 2299
Email: books@troubador.co.uk
Web: www.troubador.co.uk/matador
Twitter: @matadorbooks

ISBN 978-1-80313-702-5

British Library Cataloguing in Publication Data.
A catalogue record for this book is available from the British Library.

Printed and bound in Great Britain by 4edge Limited
Typeset in 11pt Minion Pro by Troubador Publishing Ltd, Leicester, UK

Matador is an imprint of Troubador Publishing Ltd

For Layla.
I hope you grow to enjoy poetry as much as I do.

CONTENTS

INTRODUCTION

GO ON – WRITE ME A POEM!

Well, ever since I was in Mrs Huggins' class, aged four, back in 1962, I have always loved poetry and had great fun making up simple rhymes – but then discovered you don't even need to make them rhyme! Poetry is about getting your feelings down in a special, entertaining way; like making music with a pencil!

During my teaching career, helping children to write poetry was SO rewarding. This, therefore, is where my little book comes in… Here are some of the types of poetry that the children and I played around with. I thought it would be useful to group them according to topics and then there's no excuse for not having a go yourselves!

It might, of course, be a handy tool for teachers to turn to when their brains are too tired to think of some reasonable examples!

Suitable for seven-year-olds to seventy-year-olds, and beyond, there are no hard and fast rules!

Poetry is FREEDOM! Do what you want! Have fun!

ANCIENT GREEKS

Whenever we go back to Greece, we are welcomed like old friends. People as warm as their sunshine...

ACROSTIC
Grand white buildings
Rise up from the beautiful islands
Even the cats are sleek and elegant
Every city has a history
Kalimera – their friendly greeting.
Sunsets so stunning across the turquoise seas.

RHYME
Medusa
Fearsome woman
Her face a shiny green
The most evil monster you have ever seen.
Flashing red eyes
Writhing snakes for hair

She would turn you to stone with just one stare.
Yet Perseus searched
In that gloomy cave
He was so scared, but very brave.
He used his shield so shiny and bright
Then struck a blow with all his might
Her scream was terrible
But she dropped dead
He used this trophy
As a terrible force
To protect all those he loved of course!

ALLITERATION
Massive monster Minotaur makes men into meals; menacing mouth munching morsels manically.
Hurry Hermes – how high and happily he hovers!
Persephone patiently picks pomegranates.
Icarus idiotically ignores information!

KENNING
Minotaur
Man eater
Maze beater
Roar maker
Life taker

Olympics
Look how fast they are!
Look how far they jump!
Look how strongly they throw!

Running!
Running so far!
Running so far in a day!
Running so far in a day to carry a message!
(The first marathon)

Olympics
The crowd waits expectantly
Everyone holds their breath
The sleek, tanned athlete
Powders his hands
Picks up the discus
And spins slowly
Controlled
Then faster and faster
Till he is just a blur
At last it is released
And lands with a distant thud
The applause is deafening…

Athenians
Believed in fairness
Education for most but
Women kept at home!

Spartans
Boys became soldiers
Girls also allowed to fight
War was everything!

What Did We Get from the Ancient Greeks?
Democracy to make things fair
Philosophy to make you stop and stare
Theatre to make you laugh and cry
Mathematics to help you reason why
Olympic Games inspire us to keep fit
Bringing nations together because of it

Pictures of Greece Today
Whitewashed houses
Yawning, slim, hungry cats
Deep blue seas
Rainbow-coloured sun hats
Soft feta cheese
Souvlaki beef on skewers
Delicious pastries on a tray
Gentle music playing all day
People dancing in long lines
Richly embroidered outfits
Show beautiful designs
Kind respectful people
Who greet you with "Yassou"
Nothing is ever a problem
Just a welcome for you!

AUTUMN

*My favourite time of year. My daughter
and I collected over 500 conkers once...*

FREE VERSE
Vintage sunshine
Flooding the afternoon garden,
With soft warmth.
Dozy bees glued to the lavender
Hopeful of pollen left behind.
Last-minute butterflies
Settle on the crusty Buddleja bush
Clinging on to summer memories
Fading fast.
Smooth conkers, nearly ripe
Just splitting their thick, green, spiky cases.
Silky swallows almost gone,
Lining rooftops, ready to journey south.
The last rose petals scattered in the sudden gusts of wind
Dropping most untidily in the rough grass.

Translucent horse chestnut leaves
Giving in to rustiness.
Almost time to hibernate,
Almost time to turn back the clocks,
Almost the end of summer.

(2)
Rough cut grass.
Misty mornings.
Amber-coloured dahlias.
Swollen apples; unpicked and shiny.
Chillier air.
Earlier lamp lighting.

(3)
Penmaenmawr 2018. October.
The sea spread out like blue silk
Rippling between the darker land
Perfect, breathtaking, uninterrupted
At this moment
Until silent birds wheeled gracefully
From one side of the bay to the other,
Low autumnal sunshine glanced
Off each sparkling wave
The beach lonely save for occasional walkers
But so beautiful, smooth, clean, perfect.
Dai closing up the creaky shutters
And taking down the sun-faded postcards
From the beach cafe window.
Time to pack away
Till next year.

KENNINGS

Flycatcher
Heather burrower
Slime trailer
Web spinner
Nut cracker
Leaf dropper
Gnat catcher
Sky soarer
Pond cooler
Sun stealer
Cloud gatherer
Autumn.

ACROSTIC

Amber glowing acorns
Underneath fragile saffron leaves
Trees turn to red and gold
Undressed by the wilder winds
Misty mornings
Nights drawing in

HUMOROUS RHYME

"Give us that conker
It's bigger than mine!"
"Go on then have it
It's absolutely fine!"
"Bet you baked it in the oven
To make it real hard,
And tested it out
In your own back yard!"

"Well you'll have to give it back
After school
And leave the string in
That's the rule!"

ALLITERATION
Worried wasps wearily wander
Tripping tipsily towards toppled timber
Crystal coloured cobwebs carefully collect crane flies
Children cheerfully choose chunky chestnuts

HAIKU
Crunchy golden leaves
Scattered across the park's path
Such fun to stamp on!

Golden September
And the swallows get ready
For African flights

Squirrels so busy
Collecting nuts to bury
Deeply in soft earth

Autumn richness gives
Promise of exciting times
To brighten dark days.

CHRISTMAS

So many poems and songs have been written already, but it never fails to be a special time amidst even the darkest of days…

FREE VERSE
Tree stands silently
Strong
Smelling
Subtly sensational
Tiny lights
Cheer
Inky black nights
Each trinket
Lovingly placed
On the very edge
Of spiky branches
The angel
Stares serenely
And smiles.

ALLITERATION

Silent stable, so safe under soft starlight
Magical moments make memories
Flimsy fairy, fragile and fluttering
Pretty present parcelled in pink paper

ACROSTIC (RHYMING)

Carry the baby along the dusty road
Heavy for the donkey, its precious load
Ring out those bells tonight
It's such clear starlight
Shining for all to see
The magic of his majesty
Marvel at the baby in the straw
Angels and shepherds at the draughty door
Special gift to all, rich and poor.

KENNINGS (RHYMING)

Carol singer
Bell ringer
Cracker puller
Feeling fuller
Joke teller
Candle seller
Mistletoe kisser
Pantomime hisser
Santa writer
Child delighter

HAIKU

In the deep dark night
A special child was given
To light up the world

Born in a stable
On a manger of rough wood
To give hope for good

The poor shepherds gazed
Three wise men knelt before him
And the angels sang

Animals lay soft
And kept the tiny room warm
Strong, silent, quiet

What joy he would bring
To the lives of so many
Great, small, young and old.

FREE STRUCTURED VERSE

I went to bed
Straight away
Before Santa's lights
Lit up our path.
I'm sure I heard
The tinkling of a bell!
Snuggle down more
But one eye open
Just a little bit.

A creaky stair,
The swish of a door.
My handle turned.
Now eyes shut tight
For ages…
And suddenly it's morning
Light flooding in
The presents are crammed
At the foot of my bed.
I missed him again…

COVENTRY

This place has been my home since 1983 and I am proud of all that the city stands for – its history, its welcoming traditions and its rich cultures.

ACROSTIC
Cathedral shell of the ruined old joined to the bright hopeful new.
Only two city gates left out of twelve but
Vivid rich colours of flags and ribbons welcome and
Everyone can find kindness here,
Now living up to our 'Two Tone' history.
Three splendid spires silhouetted at sunset above the
River Sherbourne tucked secretly away.
Yesterday's legends still important today.

LIMERICK

There was a lady called Godiva
Who was a very keen horse rider
She took off her clothes
As everyone knows
But peeping Tom espied her!

FREE VERSE WITH STRUCTURE

You can still **see**
The old city wall
In between the sleek apartments,
A reminder of a medieval past
You can still **hear** about
Lady Godiva, our famous hero.
The city clock makes people stare
As the hour chimes
And the creaky wooden figure circles its face.

You can still **feel** the rhythms of so much music
Black and white Ska, African drums, up-tempo bhangra,
Irish jigs, classical Indian dance
Played in our homes
Echoing through the streets.

You can still **smell** the factories and cars
But sweetened by rose gardens
And large green spaces of freshly mown grass
Fragrant bushes and shrubs
Soothe the senses and awaken memories in our tree-lined
Memorial Park.

You can still **taste** food from every culture
Rich, moist, tempting,
Hot, colourful, spicy, creamy
On simple street carts or fancier restaurants,
A fabulous assortment reflecting its people.

ALLITERATION
Godiva...
Bold, beautiful, with boundless bravery,
Caring, comforting, confronting
Quietly questioning
Single-minded, strong and stubborn.

KENNINGS
Coventry...
Bomb taker
History maker
Phoenix riser
War despiser
Peace giver
Life liver.

RHYMING VERSE
Old Cathedral
Only the walls still stand proud
I stand in silence, my head bowed
The sun finds ancient window glass
Remembering what came to pass
I can almost hear the engine's drone
As I pause here all alone
Imagining the roof, all on fire

Shattered stones, blackened spire.
Yet out of the rubble comes bright hope
A charred wooden cross to help us cope
Another made of strong roof nails
This heartfelt message never fails.

New Cathedral
How light
How bright
How full of joy
So much to celebrate and enjoy.
A huge screen carved with angels and saints
The Baptistry window like a box of paints.
Long strips of glass along the side
Created with love and looked at with pride.
The awe-inspiring tapestry
Comfort and power for all to see.
A feeling of strength and a brave new start,
A proud gem in Coventry's heart.

DINOSAURS

I have always loved anything to do with dinosaurs!
Fierce, fast – FASCINATING!

ACROSTIC
Dangerous creatures roaming so free
Imagine how much taller they were than me!
Not all of them would eat other creatures
Oh look at Stegosaurus's crazy features!
Some say they died because of ice
And others reckoned they were just not nice
Unusual names and curious looks
Remember the facts, look in the books.
Scary!

HAIKU

Steaming blood dripping
From its enormous white teeth
Some small creature caught.

Cold huge bones lying
Buried deep for years and years
Still fearsome today.

Were some of them kind?
Just gentle heavy giants,
Lumbering but calm?

KENNINGS

Flesh tearer
Ground thumper
Tooth sharpener
Eye blinker
Tail swisher
Claw stretcher
Roar thunderer
Terror giver.

FREE VERSE

Hear the mighty roar
Feel the ground shake
Smell the terrible breath
Taste the danger in the air
See the monster – beware!

ALLITERATION

Terrifying Tyrannosaurus tears with terrible teeth.
Really remarkable reptiles roar ridiculously
Find fantastic footprints forever.

DIWALI

*Don't you just love this gorgeous festival giving out so much
joy, light and fabulous food!*

ACROSTIC

Decorating houses with divas and Rangoli patterns,
Idols of Lakshmi and Ganesh everywhere.
Watching gorgeous fireworks against an inky black sky.
Always fun, always lively,
Lights of every colour and style
India leads the celebrations which now take place all over
the world.

PATTERNED FREE VERSE

Did you see the divas
Decorating everybody's windowsill?
Did you smell the fireworks
Exploding in a garden nearby?
Did you hear the children

Playing with their cousins?
Did you taste the gorgeous sweets
So sugary and rich?
Did you touch the smooth bright silk
Of your Mum's new sari?

EGYPTIANS

How lovely would it be to visit the pyramids and touch
their sun-soaked walls so full of stories...

FREE VERSE
Great sun touching every stone
Of every pyramid
The Sphynx, casting huge deep shadows
On the smooth sand.

The giant crumbling structures
Dwarf the camel drivers,
As the dust billows from the animals' hooves.
Everything here is huge.

KENNINGS
Camels
Sand shifter
People carrier

Water storer
Dust snorter

Pyramids
Tomb hider
Cold keeper
Treasure bearer
Secret breaker
Mummy burier
Story teller

Mummy
Life muffler
Bondage maker
King suffocater
Voice silencer
Energy sapper
Legend maker

ACROSTIC (RHYMING)
Elegant shiny-faced masks
Glinting on top of huge still casks.
Yellow walls crumbling away
Precious stones didn't see light of day.
Tutankhamun was here to stay

ALLITERATION
Serene silhouettes set in the silent sunset.
Cautious camels cantering carefully.
Motionless mummies, marvellous but menacing.
Grim glaring gods guarding graves.

HAIKU

Canopic Jars
Cold grey-sided jars
Topped with blank-eyed fitted lids.
Dark contents hidden

Shabti
Silent, arms folded
Obedient to the last
Waiting to serve still

Sarcophagus
Grand locked precious box
Bejewelled and richly engraved
The king's resting place

FREE VERSE WITH STRUCTURE
Dig deep and uncover the dead
From their dusty tombs
Dig deep and sweep away
Years of sand and grime
Dig deep and polish the old jewels
In the gloomy sunset
Dig deep to peer back
Into the echoes of time.

MINIBEASTS

Okay, so I scream when I see a spider!
Ridiculous, I know, because they do nothing but good...

FREE VERSE (NO RHYME)

Wasps

No one likes us
They all make a fuss
If we get near them
They flap us away
What they don't realise
Is how good we are
For the plants
For the environment
We are just as important as bees
So there!

Ants
So tiny yet so busy
They are never still
Or lonely it seems.
They gather together
To get the jobs done
Organised
Like an army.
Who tells them what to do?

RHYMING VERSE
Caterpillar
Crawled out slowly from a tiny white egg
Fur standing on end near each tiny leg.
It eats and eats every day
Munching on everything in its way.
Then when it becomes very big and fat
It slows right down and sits still, just like that.
For weeks it seems to do nothing at all
Till a gorgeous butterfly surprises us all.

ALLITERATION
Spiders
So small so spindly
Sticky silk softly sways
Sensing something so satisfying

ACROSTIC

Spider silk is so strong
Prey is caught before very long
Incredibly useful – they gobble up flies
Did you know they have eight eyes?
Every web takes an hour to make
Really beautiful patterns without a mistake.

KENNINGS (RHYMING)

Snail

Slow creeper
Time keeper
Silent feeler
Lettuce stealer
Slime trailer
Spiral tailor

KENNINGS (NO RHYME)

Worm

Hole maker
Dirt taker
Path designer
Mud dragger
Air bringer
Earth fertiliser

HAIKU (RHYMING)

Wasps

Brightly coloured pest
Yellow and black shiny vest
Never seem to rest!

Bees
Softly dancing bee
Show me what you can now see
Honey made for me!

HAIKU (NO RHYME)
Beetle
Shiny black armour
Covers its busy body
Look out antennae!

NORTH AMERICA

*Such a mix of lifestyles, animals and scenery –
with unexpected history!*

ACROSTIC

Never go just for Disneyland!
Awesome lakes the size of seas
Missouri river surrounded by trees.
Endless highways for your limousine
Rocky mountains, grand canyons; must be seen.
Indians the first Americans, with rich history
Cowboys still ride in rodeos you see.
An amazing continent you'll agree!

SKIPPING RHYME
M i s s i s s i p p i
m i, crooked letter, crooked letter, i
crooked letter, crooked letter, i p p i
(skip 'doubles' when you say 'crooked letter'!)

North American animals
Beavers that build and bears that roar,
Alligators that terrify and moose that snore.
Armoured armadillos that roam at night,
The monarch butterfly – a beautiful sight.
Arctic wolves need not be feared
The hummingbird – mosquito-like – so weird!
The caribou stands tall and proud
The Gila monster is sleepy, not loud
There are ferrets, raccoons, opossums, bullfrogs,
pronghorn, antelopes, coyote, wild dogs!

STRUCTURED RHYME
Grizzly Bear
Have you seen the Grizzly
Standing tall and proud?
Have you heard his roar
So terribly loud?
Have you felt the ground tremble as he runs?
Have you smelt the smoke from the hunters' guns?

KENNINGS
Bear
Ground trembler
Mountain plodder
Salmon catcher
Speed gatherer
River swimmer
Man eater!

HAIKU

Alligators
Wide open jaw smiles
But don't trust them show respect
He's watching you now!

Hummingbirds
Colourful yet small
Tremendous tiny wings beat
Fast in one big blur.

Arctic Wolf
Silver grey, handsome
Not quite as fierce as brown bears,
Roaming the cold slopes.

Caribou
They lift their huge heads
Displaying such strong antlers
And long winter beards.

Blue Jay
Sleek blue patterned back
A tufted plume and white vest,
So loud and busy.

Raccoons
Wearing a black mask
Like a small naughty robber
Raiding old trash cans.

ALLITERATION

Meandering magnificent Mississippi
Fantastic Florida, forever fabulous.
Energetic eagles effortlessly escaping.

New York, never noiseless,
California, constantly colourful and crazy,
Washington's wonderful White House.

STRUCTURED VERSE

Native Americans
Listen
To the stories
The old chieftain tells
Smoking his pipe
Inside his skin tipi

Listen
To the thud
Of the drums from afar
Beating the rhythm
Of the ancient war dance

Listen
To the songs
Carried by the wind
Sung around the campfires
Echoed through the valleys

Listen
To the names
Of the old old tribes
Sayings passed down
Through the ages

Listen
To the breeze
Blowing through the dream catcher
Keeping the children safe
In the dead of night.

RAINFORESTS

Colourful, fascinating and mind-blowing.
Let's look after them.

RHYME
Warm heavy atmosphere
Everything so ALIVE here.
Rain dripping from every tree,
Sometimes as quietly as can be.
Waterfalls splash to create rainbows
Creatures' bright colours all on show.
Lazy sloths swing from branch to branch,
Haunting music puts us in a trance.

ACROSTIC
Read
All about
It!
Not one creature is safe

From extinction
Only humans can
Reduce the devastation
Even the smallest creature lost is
Such a
TRAGEDY!

ALLITERATION
Rushing, raging rivers roaring,
Slippery surfaces, so sumptuous,
Large leathery leaves lean languidly,
Busy beautiful birds boldly banquet
On intoxicating insects so infinitely interesting…

HAIKU
"Why have they cut them?"
The children cried in horror
Seeing forest clearings

Another poor creature
Becoming extinct today
Stop it! We must say!

HAIKU (RHYMING)
Wet, warm; wonderful
Rich with life for all to see
Beautiful canopy

KENNINGS (RHYMING)
Air giver
Life liver

Home provider
Insect hider
Bird keeper
Water seeper
Sloth prowler
Monkey howler
Frog leaper
Snake peeper

STRUCTURED FREE VERSE
Rainforest facts
Drip drip
The raindrop takes
Ten minutes to reach the floor
Drip drip
They make waterfalls on every leaf
Drip drip
The animals drink
The flowers can glisten in the pools of sunlight
Drip drip
The lake is filled
And rises steadily
Drip drip
The trees have heard it for 2,000 years
Drip drip
It waters the plants that give us
Medicine and hope
Drip drip
250 centimetres of rain (at least)
Every year!

ROMANS

They left their roads and impressive remains,
but they weren't always welcome...

ACROSTIC
Red shields with gold patterns
Orcus – god of death
Mosaic floors beautifully decorated their houses
Augustus, the first Roman emperor
Numerals that we still see on clocks today
Soldiers highly trained to move and fight together

STRUCTURED FREE VERSE
So strong
So clever and skilled
So organised in battle
So many straight roads
So much that they achieved in 400 years
Nevertheless
So many Britons hated them!

RHYMING VERSE
questions
Were they always so serious, so determined and strong?
Did they ever mean to stay for so long?
Were they constantly fierce and up for a fight?
Did they behave well, and were they polite?
Were they ever more gentle or even just kind?
Did they treat with respect the things they might find?
Were they ever just happy to be on our land?
Did they expect people to obey every command?
Were they ever quite grateful to be living here?
Or did they make all Britons live completely in fear?

ALLITERATIVE RHYMING VERSE
Boudica
Brave and beautiful
Bold and strong
Battled for the Iceni
All day long
Cunning and courageous
Crafty and clever
Celts gathered round her
Their queen forever.

KENNINGS (RHYMING)
Romans
Road builder
Villa maker
Heat provider
Life taker

Mosaic designer
Concrete mixer
Arch constructor
Calendar fixer.

HAIKU
Tall standard-bearers
Leading highly trained legions
To fight and to win

Their clothes seemed so wrong
For the cold British weather
Sandals letting in rain.

SCHOOL

Sometimes we love it, sometimes we hate it –
but we all have to go!

ACROSTIC (RHYMING)
So it's great to be back
Carrying on, keeping track.
Hope everyone will still be the same,
Oh just to hear you call my name!
Only a term left to work and play,
Let's make the most of every day!

KENNINGS
The Schoolchild
Lesson learner
House point earner
Classroom worker
Playground jumper
Spelling scribbler

Number cruncher
Sandwich muncher
Paint splasher
Computer crasher
Netball shooter
Goal saver
Library reader
Follow my leader

ALLITERATION
School so silent sometimes seems sad on Sundays.
Monday's marvellous music makes magic in my mind.
Taking time on Tuesday to try tennis.
What wonders we witnessed on Wednesday!
Thinking things through on Thursday.
Friday feels fantastic.
Soccer on Saturday so sensational!

QUESTION AND ANSWER
What are you doing?
Rubbing it out.
Why?
Because it's rubbish!
Who says?
I do!
But are you going to start again?
Can't be bothered!
Why don't I help you?
It's not yours.
But maybe I can give you ideas?
But they're not mine!

Shall I go then?
If you like.
Why are you smiling?
I've just had an idea.
Can you write it down?
No that's the problem.
Well can you say it?
Yes in my head!

STRUCTURED VERSE
School today
It's Monday and I'm scared
'Cos there's a spelling test
School today
It's Tuesday and I'm worried
'Cos I don't know my tables
School today
It's Wednesday and I'm nervous
'Cos it's swimming and I'm going in the deep end.
School today
It's Thursday and I'm frightened
'Cos I've got to stand up and read in assembly
School today
It's Friday and I'm happy!
It all turned out okay!

HAIKU (RHYMING)
Teachers who are kind
Never leave you far behind
They improve your mind!

Make the most of school
That must be your golden rule
Or you are a fool!

HAIKU (NO RHYME)
It's so very calm
Look how they concentrate still
Scratching pens neatly

RHYME
Love to dance
Love to sing
Love to read
Love to create
Love to act with my best mate
Love to cook
Love to glue
But in Maths I haven't a clue!

LIMERICK
There was a young teacher from Eastern Green
With the fastest car I've ever seen
He raced it right out of our playground
Spinning the tyres with a screeching sound
He's late for his tea I'll be bound!

SPACE

Who isn't fascinated by space? The final frontier?!

FREE
Beautiful blue planet,
Half hidden from sight,
Part lit by a generous sun.
The moon's surface in comparison,
Softly lumpy and grey,
Lifeless, cool and so far from home.

FREE (RHYMING)
Gradually lightening sky,
Laced with pink and gold.
Rocket cold and oh so high,
Astronauts – so bold!

Gently rumbling, engines awake,
Smoke billowing on all sides.

Trembling earth starts to quake
The most thrilling of all rides!

KENNINGS
The Rocket
Engine growler
Cloud splitter
Flame shooter
Frontier breaker
Astronaut keeper
Risk taker
Trail blazer
Star shaker

ALLITERATION
Space
Empty, everlasting, eternal.
Space so silent.
Far reaching, frozen forever,
Velvety vision, vanishing valleys.
Mysterious, marvellous, menacing moon,
Petite purple planets, perfectly placed.
Distant deep darkness,
Luminous low-level light.

STRUCTURED/FREE
Fly me to the moon
Fly me to the moon
On a sleek rocket ship.
Fly me to the planet Mars,
An even longer trip.

Fly me to another galaxy,
Far away beyond our star.
Fly me to see the gorgeous colours,
Of a new nebula.

HAIKU
1. Distant bright starlight
Shining through even thickest clouds
Mysterious sight

2. Strange green faces look
Out from their silver rocket.
Will we welcome them?

3. Is there anybody there?
Sounds echo across empty space.
Did someone answer?

ACROSTIC (RHYMING)
Space – the final frontier
Perhaps our chance to be freer?
Adventurous types are what we need
Courageous and willing to succeed –
Even my grandma, if she's up for it!

SPRING

When life begins again.
Warmth, growth, movement and MUD!

RHYMING VERSE
The bird stood on the wooden deck
Of the brand-new feeder
Ate two mealworms in one peck
After all he was the leader!
His bright red breast stuck out so proud
Puffed out fluffily, made to look big,
Listen as he sings out loud,
"I don't care a jot, I don't give a fig!"

FREE VERSE (STRUCTURED)
A
Single snowdrop
Appears so suddenly
Overnight it almost seems

Giving out hope in January
Bravely nodding its head in the breeze.

FREE VERSE (LIMITED RHYME)
Can't see
The nests that are hidden
In the tightly packed hedge.
Sparrows and robins flutter excitedly
Around its edge.
Tempting to look?
No definitely not!
Just imagine the nest
With its cool blue eggs
Laid gently to rest.

RHYMING VERSE
Going for a welly walk
Down here in the park
Squishing through the mud
Until its almost dark
Best thing is when your boot
Gets sucked in and stuck!
Then you overbalance
And go splat right in the muck!
Sometimes the muddy water
Slops all over the top
Your socks get soaking wet
And we yell, "Hey you lot – STOP!"
But all they do is giggle
And race right on ahead
Better have a bath before you go to bed!

KENNINGS
Weather warmer
Tadpole tamer
Bud opener
Leaf uncurler
Egg cracker
Light spreader
Seed splitter
Lamb springer
Hope bringer!

HAIKU
Crocuses spread out
In carpets of such colour
Over the pale grass

Birds are so busy
Collecting twigs and paper
Grand nest designers!

ACROSTIC (RHYMING)
So much activity in my garden today
Perhaps it's time to come and play.
Robins, sparrows, wrens and thrushes
In every corner of trees and bushes
Now is the time to dig and to sow
Give thanks for the rain to make it all grow.

SUMMER

Lazy, crazy, hazy days, full of fun in the sun...

ACROSTIC (RHYMING)
So at last the sun is in the sky,
Umbrella's up, but not to keep dry!
Mowers hum, buzzards creak above us all,
Marvellous ice cream for big and small.
Everyone's hot, sweaty and lazy,
Really want that fly to stop driving me crazy!

ALLITERATION
Sweet summery sounds so soothing,
Mowers making methodical marks,
Warm white washing waving wildly on a windy Wednesday.
Thick thudding thunder threatens!

STRUCTURED VERSE (NO RHYME)

Is it time?
To pack my case?
To go to the beach?
To get an ice cream?
To fly my kite?
To get my swimming stuff on?
To buy a fishing net?
To swing in a hammock?
To squint at the swallows?
To splodge on the suncream?
To choose some cool shades?
Is it time?
For SUMMER?

RHYMING VERSE

Whenever we go to the beach…
There's sand in my toes,
Flies up my nose!
There's grit in the bread,
Eat lollies instead!
The towel's dripping wet
Not finished splashing yet!
The seagull's so mean!
Nothing is clean.
There's sandcastles galore,
Rockpools to explore.
There's laughter,
There's fun,
We're so grateful for sun!

LIMITED RHYME

Sports' Day

I really ran so fast
But I still turned out the worst
They patted my head
And said, "Oh, never mind."
I just can't stand it
When they're being kind.
Next year I'll train
I'll keep up with the pace,
But hey… I've got a chance
It's the SLOW bicycle race!

LIMERICKS

There was a swimmer from Carlisle
Who'd been in the sea for a while,
His head was sunburnt
So a lesson he's learnt
That careless swimmer from Carlisle!

There was a big seagull from Blackpool
Who thought he looked rather cool
He strutted up and down
All around town
That big-headed seagull from Blackpool.

HAIKU

Seagulls

Always so noisy
They snaffle your fish and chips
If you don't watch out!

Puffins

Neat with a sharp beak
Which holds tiny dripping fish
Some fall on bright feet.

KENNINGS

Summer sun

Sweat pourer
Siesta snorer
Eye dazzler
Grass scorcher
Energy sapper
Skin tanner
Holiday planner!

SEA

Wild and wonderful, different every minute,
every hour, every day.

ALLITERATION
Serenely slipping sideways,
Cool, constantly changing,
Deceptively deeper, down, down, down.
Shadows shifting shapely along the shore.

Perfect puffins peck persistently,
Stately seagulls soar, selfishly snapping at seashells,
Cold crabs career courageously capering round calm corners
in the cove.

HAIKU
Frilly foam tumbling
Speedily chasing along
Sinking breathlessly.

RHYMING COUPLETS
An invisible hand,
Steadied on the land,
Paints silky green and blue,
Grey, white, every hue,
Capturing the light
Bringing ocean into sight
Even on a white
Woodchip wall.

ACROSTIC
Sometimes menacing
Ever moving
Always mesmerising

Silvery, shimmering, reflecting gentle moonlight.
Eerie, never silent.
Advancing and retreating, never still.

KENNINGS (RHYMING)
Foam maker
Fish waker
Rock licker
Oil slicker
Pebble shifter
Sand sifter
Mood lifter

QUESTION AND ANSWER
Can you see the sea yet?
Only a mile to go I bet.

Is the tide in?
If I see it first, I win!
Look, is that our beach?
Yes, it's almost in reach
Can we run onto the sand?
Yes, but hold my hand!
Can I get my feet wet?
No, not yet!

FREE VERSE FIRST PERSON
Oh, it's so cold!
I'm just going in
Up to my knees first
Ouch, that jagged rock hurt!
What's that…
Swimming round my toes?
Mind out for jellyfish,
I kind of like seaweed
But not when it's slimy
Round my ankle.
There, I'm ready
To jump – over – that – WAVE!
It makes you dizzy,
I can taste the salt.
I'm floating – YES
If my feet can't touch the sand
I'm really
Going
To
PANIC!

VICTORIANS

A fascinating time in history... but would you have liked to have lived like they did?

FREE VERSE

The Schoolroom

The schoolroom is silent
Save for the scratching of pens.
Beautiful handwriting
Curved and intricately joined.
Unwashed heads bowed over heavy-lidded desks
The smell of ink and carbolic soap in the air.
She walks purposefully between them all
Heavy skirts brushing their scruffy boots.
Then a cry at the back of that dim room
Ink has been smudged
His work ruined.
The birch rod trembles in her white hand.

KENNINGS
Chimney Sweep
Fire watcher
Soot gatherer
Chimney climber
Smoke smeller
Brush stretcher
Dirt collector
White-toothed smiler
Barefoot scrambler
Black nail grabber
Rag wearer
Tear hider
Comfort searcher

RHYMING COUPLETS
The Alleyway
A tall figure stands at the end of the alley
Don't look at him, don't dilly dally
Black top hat and a heavy cape
Do not stare, do not gape
The fog swirls round him, a mysterious figure
Do not speak, or nervously snigger.
He taps his cane upon the ground
The whole street echoes with the sound.
Who is he? Don't ask, don't pry
Just leave him be, just pass him by!

Woollen Mills

Rattle rattle click clack
Stay on time, stay on track.
Crouch down, lie on the ground
Do not moan or make a sound.
Tie the knots and pick the wool
Drag the bins when they are full.
Do not stop, get over here
Smack your legs, clip your ear.
Get up early, go home late,
Got to put bread on your mother's plate.
This is your life, do not complain
No one to turn to when you're in pain.
Get through the day and sleep cold at night
No crumb of comfort, no end in sight.

HAIKU

Crowded old houses
Clustered together tightly
Stinking and draughty

Ragged poor children
Barefoot on the wet cobbles
Searching for old bread

At the other side
Of the very same city
Lie huge posh houses

All kinds of playthings
Rocking horses, pretty dolls
Brightly coloured tops

Delicious rich food
No thought for the poor children
Crying on the streets.

ALLITERATION
Colourful Christmas cards
Huge heavy hats
Strict schoolmasters swinging sticks
Incredible inventors investigating ideas.

ACROSTIC
Very prim and proper
Inventive
Carefully dressed
Terrific twirling tin tops
Oliver Twist!
Religious
Imaginative writers
Accomplished
Never naughty
Strict

VOLCANOES

Awe-inspiring, shocking, yet always thrilling.

KENNINGS
Mountain growler
Rock melter
Flame maker
Lava spewer
Orange dribbler
Night lighter
Star blocker
Smoke teaser
Dust settler
Life freezer

ALLITERATION
Violent, vivid, vicious volcano,
Sudden, steaming, swirling surprise.
Ferocious, fiery flames flickering,

Rumbling, roaring, rolling, reaching.
Groaning, gathering, growing, gushing,
Covering completely.
Still, sad; silently steaming.

ACROSTIC (RHYMING)
Vesuvius, a sleeping giant people say.
Omnipresent, sinister mood; even today.
Let its awful history slowly unfold,
Continue the legend, the truth will be told.
At its heart lies a molten core,
No one can tell, or even be sure
Of the next disastrous eruption.

STRUCTURED RHYMING
Standing majestic in the evening light,
Still, heavy, an imposing sight.
Brown rock carved with patterns deep,
Who said the volcano was still asleep?
Suddenly, without warning, flames brighten the sky,
As a lone seabird swoops nearby.
The smoke curls around the very top,
No way anyone can make it stop.
Fire appears, raging high,
The sound of lava bubbling nearby.
A mighty groan erupts from its heart,
The villagers must surely depart.
Away from the terrifying flow,
Of molten rock, all aglow…

HAIKU
See the redness ooze
From the craggy mountain
Bubbling and hissing

Sliding quickly down
Dust and ash covering all
The greedy monster

Then nothing is left
When lava cools and hardens
Life frozen forever.

Pompei
There they were
Going about their usual lives:
Selling their goods
Cleaning their houses
Drinking their wine
Eating their delicious food.
Children shouting and playing happily
Just a normal day…
Then far in the distance
A low rumble was heard.

WINTER

Winter Wonderland... more than just a Christmas card!

ALLITERATION
Wild winds whistling, worrying weary workers
Cold colours carefully creeping close to craggy clouds.
Rouge ragged robins refusing rest,
Small snowflakes softly slipping onto the streets.

HAIKU
Snowflakes fall softly
Turning everything round us
Into white stillness.

Tiny house sparrow
Feather-deep in snow so thick
Surely must find food.

Fog smothers the street
Eerie in a yellow light,
Like fingers spreading

Sunset turns the ice
Into a fiery wonder.
Opposites attract!

KENNINGS
Water halter
Wind whistler
Breath taker
Ice maker
Light snatcher
Cold catcher
Snow muffler
Sneeze snuffler.

ACROSTIC
Wild winds blow the snow across the mountain tops.
Inky black skies.
Night comes earlier each day.
Trembling lone leaf left on a dark branch.
Every small creature
Rolls up into its winter ball.

When
It's
Never
Too
Early for
Rudolph!

FREE VERSE

My fingers
Are so cold
They might
Snap off
One by one.
My toes
Don't belong
To me,
They aren't there –
Even when
I stamp
Ever so
Hard!

RHYME

Down in the playground
We race to get out first
The air is so cold
I think my lungs will burst!
Someone's made a slide
Right beside the tree
Teachers tried to warn us
But that doesn't stop me!
Run as fast as your feet can go
Take off and slither just right
Jump off at the very end
Scream with delight!
I can do it on one foot
It's really not that hard –
Spread your arms, you're flying –
Beware, be on your guard!

WOMEN

Poems about, and for, girls and, indeed, women of all ages.

ACROSTIC (RHYMING)

We remember the courage of ladies in history
Only their strength gave women victory,
Making it clear equal rights are a must
Each and every one believes this is just
Never forget how they could have been crushed.

KENNINGS

Woman

Calming comforter
Patient partner
Idea giver
Constant listener
Pain reliever
Rule maker
Risk taker

Tradition breaker
Friend keeper
Family gatherer
Career seeker
Emotion checker
Love spreader

Suffragette Colours
Green, purple and white
Women haven't always had rights.
Green, purple and white
They had to put up a fight.
Green, purple and white
Chained to the street lights.
Green, purple and white
The awful hunger strikes.
Green, purple and white
In prison in the dead of night.
Green, purple and white
Till men saw the light.

HAIKU
Do ten jobs at once
Still smiling but so tired
Still giving her love

Fighting for equality
Even in these modern times
Much work to be done.

STRUCTURED FREE VERSE

One Day

One day
The domestic jobs will really be shared
One day
Our careers will be just as important
One day
We will watch women's sport as much as men's
One day
We will stop feeling guilty about working
One day
There'll be more women presidents
One day
Wars will stop
Because they will listen to WOMEN.

ALLITERATION

My mother made me most marvellous meals
Giggling granny gave great guffaws
Girls get going!
Lovely ladies let laughter lift you
Teach tiny toddlers to try tea sets and trains
Women wonder why we want weary work.

WORLD WAR II

Future generations need to make sure that war is something to be avoided at all costs.

ACROSTIC
When will people learn
All war is evil
Remember the lessons of the past

Wasted lives,
Atrocious scenes
Retell the soldiers' bravery.

STRUCTURED FREE VERSE
Join Up!
Join up, join up!
Your country needs you!
… And your family doesn't?
Join up, join up!

Put aside your childish ways.
Time to be a man... or a woman...
Join up, join up!
Nothing to be scared of,
Just put on that smart uniform...
Join up, join up!
We will train you
But can't promise to keep you safe.
Join up, join up!
Think of the excitement
Not the horror, the deaths.
Join up, join up!
What are you waiting for?
Why are you afraid?

In the Future

In the future
When there's an argument
We won't fight
We'll sort it out
No more terrible loss of life.
In the future
If countries disagree
We'll find a way
To come to an agreement
And settle things down quickly.
In the future
We'll remember
The death, the pain, the unfairness
The young lives cut short
The destroyed cities and villages.

In the future
We'll use some common sense
And act like adults
Not children in the playground
Fighting in anger.

Remembrance
Pure white crosses standing on the hill
The words upon them remind us still
Of young lives lost before their time
No mention of terror, horror or grime.
People leave flowers, others say prayers
Only to show someone still cares.

Remember, Remember
Remember, remember the 11th of November,
Crying and suffering a lot.
I see no reason
Why all this fighting
Should ever be forgot.

November
(Like the famous poem by Thomas Hood)
No lights from the windows
No streetlamps at night
No men in our city – all gone to fight.
No sweets until Friday
No lollies to chew
No meat except sausage, just wait in the queue!
No new clothes for parties

No smart shoes for me
No roasts on Sundays – bread and dripping for tea.
No trams in the morning
No buses or trains
No umbrella to hold up, even when it rains
No end to this war
No peace is in sight
Just cuddle your loved ones in the shelter at night.

TO LAYLA FROM NANNY MEL, MARCH 2022

No apologies for this – now I am a nanny!

ACROSTIC
Look at those shining eyes
Already watching
Your expression so wise
Let's treasure these moments
Always capture the moment, for time flies.

FREE
Welcome to this world
So tiny, perfect and softly formed.
May you feel love
Hear laughter
Taste warm milk
Smell the freshness of spring
See beauty all around you!

HAIKU

Narrow pink fingers
So tiny and delicate
Instinctively grasp

Her beautiful face
With soft unblemished features
Framed with thick, dark hair

She turns and stretches
Comfortable and content
What does she dream of?

KENNINGS

Tummy gurgler
Lip purser
Leg thrasher
Foot prodder
Fist clencher
Body curler
Heart warmer
Love giver

THE HORSE CHESTNUT

And finally, this is true...

In the year 2000
She planted a conker
Shiny and new
Alongside her time capsule
For the future to view
"Of course it won't grow!" her father had said
And laughed as he shook
His handsome tanned head.
But grow it did, year upon year
She would check it secretly
Sitting by it for fear
Of missing the new leaves
Opening wide

Then twenty-one years later
The daughter – a mummy-to-be
Stood beneath that same chestnut tree.
On the day she found out
A child had started to grow
The young tree's first conker put in a show
Dropped gently to the floor
Shiny and new
And so life goes on
For me and for you.